Utah

by Patricia K. Kummer,
Capstone Press
Geography Department

Content Consultant:
Nancy N. Mathews
Social Studies Specialist
Utah State Office of Education

CAPSTONE
HIGH/LOW BOOKS
an imprint of Capstone Press

C A P S T O N E   P R E S S

818 North Willow Street • Mankato, Minnesota 56001
http://www.capstone-press.com

Library of Congress Cataloging-in-Publication Data
Kummer, Patricia K.
 Utah/by Patricia K. Kummer (Capstone Press Geography Department).
  p. cm.--(One nation)
 Includes bibliographical references and index.
 Summary: Provides an overview of the Beehive State, including its
history, geography, people, and living conditions.
  ISBN 1-56065-683-2
  1. Utah--Juvenile literature. [1. Utah.]
  I. Capstone Press. Geography Dept. II. Title. III. Series.
F826.3.K86 1998
979.2--dc21

         97-40352
          CIP
           AC

Editorial Credits: Editor, Martha E. Hillman; cover design and illustrations,
 Timothy Halldin; photo research, Michelle L. Norstad
Photo Credits:
International Stock/Wayne Alderidge, cover; Kirk Anderson, 20
One Mile Up, 4 (top)
Root Resources/James Blank, 23; Pat Wadecki, 30
Unicorn Stock Photos/James L. Fly, 4 (bottom); Jean Higgins, 16; Charles E.
 Schmidt, 33; Herbert L. Stormont, 37
Utah Travel Council, 5 (top and bottom); Frank Jensen, 9, 10, 29
Visuals Unlimited/Mark E. Gibson, 6; Joe McDonald, 12; David Matherly, 24;
 Walt Anderson, 26; Clint Farlinger, 34; John Sohlden, 40

Table of Contents

Fast Facts about Utah

State Flag

Location: In the Rocky Mountains of the western United States

Size: 84,904 square miles (220,750 square kilometers)

Population: 2,230,856 (1996 Utah Department of Employment Security)

Capital: Salt Lake City

Date admitted to the Union: January 4, 1896; the 45th state

California seagull

Sego lily

Largest cities: Salt Lake City, West Valley City, Provo, Sandy, Orem, Ogden, Taylorsville-Bennion, West Jordan, Layton, Bountiful

Nickname: The Beehive State

State animal: Rocky Mountain elk

State bird: California seagull

State flower: Sego lily

State tree: Blue spruce

State song: "Utah, We Love Thee," by Evan Stephens

Blue spruce

Chapter 1
The Greatest Snow on Earth

Utahns are proud of their snow. Utahns are people who live in Utah. The license plates on their cars say The Greatest Snow on Earth. Utahns and visitors ski, snowboard, and snowmobile on the snow in Utah.

Great Snow Beginnings

Utah's great snow begins in clouds. Clouds full of moisture move east from the Pacific Ocean. The moisture dries out as the clouds pass over hot deserts. Then the clouds reach Utah's Wasatch Mountains. The moisture left in the clouds cools. It falls as light, dry snow.

Utahns are proud of their snow.

Each year, Utah's mountains receive over 500 inches (1,270 centimeters) of powdery snow. Skiers like this snow because it is light and fluffy.

Great Skiing

Utah has 14 downhill ski resorts. Half of them are less than a one hour drive from Salt Lake City. No other major U.S. city has as many nearby ski areas.

Alta is the nation's second-oldest ski resort. Alta is southeast of Salt Lake City. It opened in 1937.

Snowbird is near Alta. Its trams can carry 100 skiers at a time. A tram is an enclosed car that moves through the air along a heavy cable. Skiers get off the trams at Hidden Peak. This mountain is 11,000 feet (3,353 meters) above sea level. Sea level is the average level of the ocean's surface.

Some resorts offer cross-country skiing. Cross-country skiers ski on trails through a countryside. Hundreds of ski trails twist through Utah's national forests.

The trams at Snowbird can carry 100 skiers at a time.

Winter Olympics 2002

Salt Lake City will host the Winter Olympic Games in 2002. The Olympic Games are sports contests between athletes from many nations.

Utah ski areas will feature more than 10 Olympic events. Some of these events are downhill skiing, ski jumping, and bobsledding. Figure skating, hockey, and other indoor events will take place at several indoor ice rinks.

Chapter 2
The Land

Utah is in the western part of the United States. It is a Rocky Mountain state. Utah's neighbors include Nevada, Idaho, Wyoming, and Colorado. They are also Rocky Mountain states.

Arizona and New Mexico border Utah to the south. These two states and Colorado meet at Utah's southeastern corner. This spot is called Four Corners. It is the only place in the United States where four states meet.

The Colorado Plateau

The Colorado Plateau covers most of eastern and southern Utah. A plateau is an area of high,

Utah is a Rocky Mountain state.

Wind and rain have shaped rocks on the Colorado Plateau into arches, bridges, and other unusual shapes.

level land. The Colorado Plateau is large. It covers parts of Utah, Colorado, Arizona, and New Mexico.

The soil of the Colorado Plateau is hard and rocky. Over time, the Colorado and Green Rivers have cut deeply into the plateau. Wind and rain have shaped the rocks into arches, bridges, and other unusual shapes.

The Great Basin

The Great Basin covers western Utah. The Great Basin is desert land. The Great Salt Lake Desert lies in the northern part of the basin. The Sevier and Escalante Deserts are in the southern part of the basin. The Great Basin receives less than five inches (13 centimeters) of rainfall each year.

Utah's lowest point is at Beaverdam Creek. Beaverdam Creek is in Utah's southwest corner. The land there is 2,000 feet (610 meters) above sea level.

The Rocky Mountains

Two Rocky Mountain ranges come together to form a V-shape in northern Utah. They are the Uinta and Wasatch ranges. These mountains receive more rain and snow than any other part of Utah. They also have the state's lowest temperatures. Temperatures there can be as low as -30 degrees Fahrenheit (-34 degrees Celsius).

The Uinta Mountains are north of the Colorado Plateau. This is the only Rocky Mountain range that runs east and west.

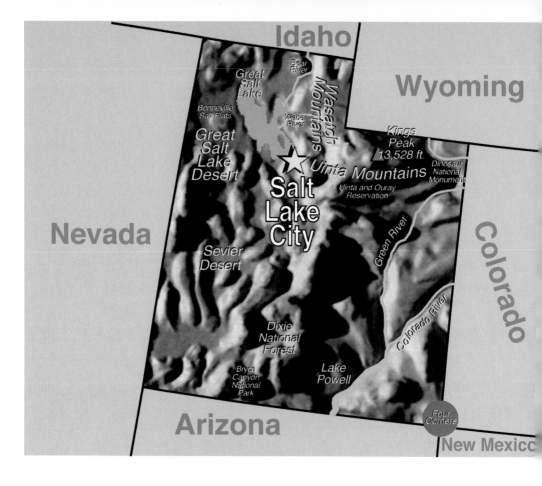

Utah's highest point is Kings Peak. It is in the Uinta Mountains. Kings Peak rises 13,528 feet (4,123 meters) above sea level.

The Wasatch Mountains are east of the Great Basin. Some of Utah's largest cities lie at the foot of the Wasatch Mountains. Salt Lake City, Orem, and Ogden are near these mountains.

Lakes and Rivers

Utah's Great Salt Lake is the largest natural lake west of the Mississippi River. This lake is in the Great Salt Lake Desert.

The Bear and Weber Rivers flow into the Great Salt Lake. No rivers flow out of the lake.

Utah Lake is the state's largest natural freshwater lake. Lake Powell is another large lake. It was formed when workers built the Glen Canyon Dam. This dam stands on the Colorado River in Arizona. Water from the river backed up behind the dam to form Lake Powell.

Plants and Animals

Pine and fir trees grow on Utah's mountains. Black bears, mule deer, and mountain lions live in the mountains.

Cactus and sagebrush grow in Utah's deserts. Rattlesnakes, Gila monsters, and desert tortoises make their homes in the deserts.

Pelicans and seagulls nest near the Great Salt Lake. Trout and bass swim in Utah's freshwater lakes and rivers.

Chapter 3
The People

Utah is one of the nation's fastest-growing states. Between 1990 and 1996, Utah's population grew by 30 percent.

The Mormon State

Sometimes Utah is called the Mormon State. A Mormon is a member of The Church of Jesus Christ of Latter-day Saints.

In 1830, Joseph Smith founded The Church of Jesus Christ of Latter-day Saints in New York. Many people did not approve of Mormon practices. They treated Mormons unfairly.

Mormons looked for religious freedom in several places. In 1847, the first Mormons settled in the area that is now Utah.

Utah is sometimes called the Mormon State. Many Mormons worship in the Mormon Temple.

Today, 65 percent of Utahns are Mormons. Salt Lake City is the world headquarters for the Church of Jesus Christ of Latter-day Saints.

European Backgrounds

About 92 percent of Utahns have European backgrounds. Some are relatives of Utah's first Mormons. Today, most Utahns have English, German, Danish, or Swedish backgrounds.

In the 1830s, Mormons began sending missionaries to other countries. A missionary is someone sent by a religious group to teach that group's faith. People from England, Denmark, Norway, and Switzerland became Mormons. Thousands of these new Mormons later moved to Utah.

Other Europeans moved to Utah in the late 1800s. Some Italians mined coal. Many Greeks mined copper and coal. Some Irish helped build railroads. Some farmers came from Germany.

Hispanic Americans

About 100,000 Utahns have Hispanic backgrounds. In the late 1800s, some Hispanics helped build railroads. Some worked in mines or factories. Many came from Latin America.

In recent years, many Mexicans have become Mormons. Some have moved to Salt Lake City and Ogden.

Native Americans

About 28,000 Native Americans live in Utah. Most of them are Ute, Goshute, Paiute, or Navajo people. Utah was named after the Utes.

Many of Utah's Native Americans live on reservations. A reservation is land set aside for use by Native Americans. The Uinta and Ouray Reservation is shared by the Uinta and Ouray people. It is the largest reservation in the state.

Other Ethnic Groups

About 43,000 Utahns are Asian Americans. Many have Japanese, Chinese, Korean, or Polynesian backgrounds. Some of their families came to Utah in the late 1800s. They helped build Utah's railroads. Many others were farmers.

About 15,000 African Americans live in Utah. A few arrived in Utah before the Mormons. They were trappers and explorers. In the late 1800s, more African Americans arrived in Utah. Many worked on railroads.

Chapter 4
Utah History

Utah's first people arrived about 12,000 years ago. They lived and hunted in the Great Basin.

The Anasazi people were Native Americans who built cliff dwellings about 1,000 years ago. Some Anasazi cliff dwellings still stand in southeastern Utah.

Other Native American groups began to arrive in the 1300s. By the 1700s, Navajo and Ute people lived in Utah. Paiute, Goshute, and Shoshone people also made homes there.

Spanish and Mexican Control

In the 1500s, Spain took control of the land that is now Utah. Captain García López de

Some Anasazi cliff dwellings still stand in southeastern Utah.

Cárdenas entered the area in 1541. He was one of the first Europeans to explore the area. It was hot. Few plants and trees grew there.

In 1821, Mexico gained independence from Spain. Mexico took control of the land that is now Utah.

American Mountain Men

In the 1820s, American mountain men entered the land that is now Utah. A mountain man is a man who makes a living trapping animals and exploring mountains.

The mountain men made trails through the Wasatch Mountains. Later, settlers would use these trails to travel through the mountains.

Mormon Settlers

In 1847, Brigham Young led Mormon people into the land that is now Utah. Young was a Mormon leader. He was looking for a place where Mormons could settle. Young's name for the area was Deseret. Deseret means honeybee in the Book of Mormon. The Book of Mormon is a Mormon religious book. Today, Utah is nicknamed the Beehive State.

Deseret was a bare, dry area when the Mormons arrived in 1847. The Mormons ate sego lily bulbs to survive. Today, the sego lily is the state flower.

The Mormons worked hard. They plowed the ground for fields. They planted crops. The farmers irrigated their crops. Irrigate means to supply dry land with water through ditches, pipes, or streams.

Grasshoppers attacked the Mormons' crops in 1848. But seagulls flew down and ate the

In 1847, Brigham Young led Mormon people into the land that is now Utah. This monument honors these settlers.

grasshoppers. The seagulls saved some of the crops. The seagull is now the state bird.

From Deseret to the Utah Territory

In 1848, the United States gained land from Mexico. This land included Deseret.

In 1850, Congress made Deseret the Utah Territory. A territory is a land area controlled by a government. A territory is not a state. Young was the first territorial governor. More than 11,000 people had already settled there.

The Utah War

Many people in the United States did not accept Mormons. The U.S. government wanted to end Mormon control in the Utah Territory. So the government named Alfred Cumming as the new territorial governor. He would take Young's place. Cumming was not a Mormon.

The U.S. government was afraid the Mormons would not accept the new governor. The government sent U.S. troops to the Utah Territory. The Mormons did not understand why the government was sending troops. They were afraid the U.S. government would not

In 1848, the United States gained Deseret from Mexico.

treat them fairly. They decided to guard their people and land.

This started the Utah War (1857-1858). There were no battles. Young tried to slow down the troops. The Mormons burned some U.S. soldiers' supplies. To be safe, many Mormons left Salt Lake City.

After a few months, Thomas Kane went to the Utah Territory. He was a government

In 1869, the first U.S. transcontinental railroad was completed in Promontory.

official and a friend of the Mormons. He explained to Young why the government had sent the troops. They would not attack. Kane brought Cumming to Salt Lake City. Young allowed Cumming to become the governor. The Mormons accepted the new governor.

Transcontinental Railroad

In 1869, the first U.S. transcontinental railroad was completed at Promontory. Transcontinental means crossing a continent.

One track began on the East Coast. The other began on the West Coast. They met at Promontory. Trains could then travel from the East Coast to the West Coast. Soon, other railroads also crossed the Utah Territory.

Statehood

By 1880, the Utah Territory had enough people for statehood. But Congress refused to make the Utah Territory a state. Some Mormon practices were against the law in the United States. In 1890, the Mormons promised to give up these practices. In 1896, Utah became the 45th state.

In 1896, Utah women won the right to vote. Women in the rest of the country did not win the right to vote until 1920.

World Wars and Depression

In 1917, the United States entered World War I (1914-1918). Utah's crops helped feed soldiers during the war. Some Utahns were soldiers.

The Great Depression (1929-1939) affected the entire country. Utah's mines

closed. Farmers lost their land. Workers lost
their jobs. The U.S. government started the
New Deal program. This program created
many projects. People took jobs working on the
projects. Many Utahns built roads and bridges.

In 1941, the United States entered World
War II (1939-1945). The U.S. government built
military bases in Utah. A special crew trained
at Utah's Wendover Army Air Base. This was
the crew that dropped an atomic bomb on
Hiroshima, Japan. An atomic bomb is a
powerful explosive that destroys large areas.
An atomic bomb leaves behind harmful
elements after it explodes. Dropping the bomb
helped end the war.

Recent Growth and Challenges

After World War II, Utah's manufacturing and
mining businesses grew. Utah companies made
steel and rockets. Uranium mines and oil fields
flourished. Uranium is a metal used in weapons
and power plants.

Tourism has grown in Utah since the 1960s.
Millions of people come to ski and to visit

In 1996, Utah celebrated its centennial. Some Utahns dressed like people did in the late 1800s.

Utah's national parks. Some of these visitors decide to move to Utah. They build homes and start new businesses.

In 1996, Utah celebrated its centennial. A centennial is a celebration that marks 100 years. Utah's centennial marked 100 years of statehood. Utahns celebrated with parades and dances. Some Utahns dressed like people did in the late 1800s.

Chapter 5
Utah Business

Service businesses employ more Utahns than other kinds of businesses. Government, tourism, and realty are leading Utah service businesses. Realty is the business of buying and selling land and buildings. Manufacturing, mining, and farming are other state businesses.

Service Businesses

About 160,000 Utahns work for the government. Hill Air Force Base in Ogden is Utah's largest employer. Many Utahns work in national parks and forests.

Every year, tourism brings about 14 million visitors to Utah. The tourists spend more

Many Utahns work in national parks and forests.

than $3 billion in Utah. The state's hotels, ski resorts, and museums earn much of this money.

Utah's growing population helps the realty business. Thousands of people buy new houses. Growing businesses buy more land.

Manufacturing

Transportation equipment is Utah's leading product. Transportation equipment moves people or objects from place to place. Thiokol Space Operations is in Brigham City. This company makes rockets for spacecraft.

The area between Salt Lake City and Provo is called Software Valley. Many companies make computer products there.

Mining

Oil is a valuable mining product in Utah. Utah's oil fields are located in the eastern part of the state.

The Kennecott Bingham Canyon Mine produces copper. Mines in central Utah produce low-sulfur coal. Low-sulfur coal is a kind of coal that pollutes less than other coal. Companies also harvest salt from the Great Salt Lake.

Much of Utah's farmland is in the north central part of the state.

Agriculture

Much of Utah's farmland is in the north central part of the state. Most of this land is irrigated.

Hay, wheat, barley, and corn are major Utah crops. Apples, peaches, pears, and cherries are leading fruits. Sugar beets and potatoes are other important crops.

Beef and dairy farms are also located in the north central part of Utah. Ranchers raise sheep in the southwestern part of the state.

Chapter 6
Seeing the Sights

Utah has many beautiful sights. Visitors explore the state's five national parks and nine national forests. They ride rafts down rivers and ski down mountains. Others enjoy Utah's cities and towns.

Salt Lake City

Salt Lake City is the state capital. Utah's lawmakers meet at the capitol. Utah copper covers this building's dome. A dome is a roof shaped like half of a globe.

Temple Square is south of the capitol. The Mormon Temple is in Temple Square. Many Mormons worship in the Mormon Temple. Only Mormons can enter the temple.

Utah has five national parks and nine national forests.

The Mormon Tabernacle and Assembly Hall are also in Temple Square. The Mormon Tabernacle is home to the Mormon Tabernacle Choir. Mormons use Assembly Hall for concerts and special events.

The Sea Gull Monument stands in front of Assembly Hall. This monument honors the seagulls that helped the first Mormon settlers in Utah.

Other Wasatch Mountain Cities

Park City hosts the Sundance Film Festival. Many new films are first shown at this festival.

Provo is south of Salt Lake City. It is home to Brigham Young University. The Mormon Church owns this college.

Ogden is north of Salt Lake City. Visitors can tour the restored Fort Buenaventura. Utah's first settlers founded Fort Buenaventura in 1846.

In Wellsville, visitors can tour the Ronald V. Jensen Living Historical Farm. Costumed workers recreate life on a Mormon farm in the early 1900s.

Northeastern Sights

Flaming Gorge National Recreation Area is in far northeastern Utah. A gorge is a deep valley with steep, rocky walls. Visitors go boating on the large lake called Flaming Gorge Reservoir.

Visitors see thousands of dinosaur fossils at Dinosaur National Monument. A fossil is the remains of an animal or plant that lived many years ago. Some scientists believe dinosaurs roamed in this area 150 million years ago.

Visitors see dinosaur fossils at Dinosaur National Monument.

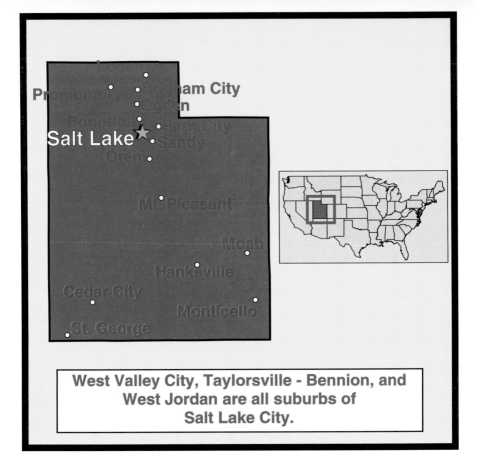

West Valley City, Taylorsville - Bennion, and West Jordan are all suburbs of Salt Lake City.

Southeastern Utah

More than 2,000 natural stone arches stand in Arches National Park. Wind and water shaped the arches over many years.

The Colorado and Green Rivers cut deep canyons in Canyonlands National Park. A canyon is a deep, narrow river valley with steep sides. Hikers walk through a twisting canyon called the Maze.

A white sandstone dome sits on top of red sandstone cliffs at Capitol Reef National Park. The dome looks like the dome of the U.S. Capitol. Butch Cassidy used Capitol Reef as a hideout. He was a bank and train robber in the early 1900s.

Monument Valley is on the Navajo Reservation. Tall, thin towers of red sandstone stand 1,000 feet (305 meters) tall.

Southwestern Utah

Southwestern Utah is called Dixie. Its hot weather reminded early Mormon settlers of the South. People also call the southern states Dixie.

Brigham Young's former winter home is located at St. George. Visitors tour his house.

The Virgin River cut a deep canyon through Zion National Park. Visitors can see fossils preserved in the canyon walls.

At Bryce Canyon National Park, the walls of the canyons are red, pink, and orange. The colors seem to change in the sunlight.

The water in the Great Salt Lake is more salty than ocean water.

Northwestern Utah

The Bonneville Salt Flats lie in the Great Salt Lake Desert. They are home to the Bonneville Speedway. Some of the fastest cars race there.

The water in the Great Salt Lake is more salty than ocean water. There is so much salt in the water that it keeps swimmers from sinking.

Golden Spike National Historic Site is at Promontory. There, visitors learn about the first transcontinental railroad.

Utah Time Line

About 10,000 B.C.—People are living in the area that is now Utah.

A.D. 400-1300—Anasazi people are farming in the Utah area.

1300-1700—Goshute, Paiute, Shoshone, Ute, and Navajo people move into the Utah area.

1541—García López de Cárdenas is one of the first Europeans to explore the Utah area.

1765—Juan Maria Rivera explores the Utah area for Spain.

1776—Francisco Atanasio Dominguez and Silvestre Velez de Escalante travel though the Utah area while trying to reach California.

1847—Brigham Young leads a group of Mormons into the Utah area. He founds Salt Lake City.

1848—The United States gains control of the Utah area and other western lands.

1850—The U.S. Congress creates the Utah Territory; the University of Utah is founded in Salt Lake City.

1857—The Utah War begins.

1869—The two parts of the transcontinental railroad meet at Promontory.

1875—Brigham Young University is founded in Provo.

1893—The Mormon Temple is completed in Salt Lake City.

1896—Utah becomes the 45th state; Utah women win the right to vote.

1906—Copper mines open in Bingham Canyon.

1934—Automobile racing begins at Bonneville Salt Flats.

1942-1945—The U.S. government moves more than 8,000 Japanese Americans to camps in Utah. The government fears they will help Japan during World War II.

1979—The Utah Jazz basketball team moves to Utah from New Orleans.

1981—Robert Redford founds the Sundance Institute, which holds the Sundance Film Festival.

1991—Deedee Corradini becomes Salt Lake City's first female mayor.

1995—Salt Lake City is chosen to host the 2002 Winter Olympics.

1996—Utah celebrates 100 years of statehood.

Famous Utahns

Roseanne Barr (1952-) Comedian and actress who starred in the television series *Roseanne*; born in Salt Lake City.

Nolan Kay Bushnell (1915-) Computer programmer who developed the first coin-operated video game (1971); born in Ogden.

Butch Cassidy (1887-1912?) Bank robber and train robber who hid out in Utah's canyon country; born George Leroy Parker in Circleville.

Philo Taylor Farnsworth (1906-1971) Inventor who gave the first demonstration of a television broadcast (1934); born in Beaver.

Donny Osmond (1958-) Singer and actor; brother of **Marie Osmond** (1959-), also a singer and actor; both born in Ogden.

Helen Zeese Papanikolas (1918-) Author and historian who wrote about ethnic groups, especially Greeks, in Utah; born in Price.

Ivy Baker Priest (1905-1975) Banker and government official who served as treasurer of the United States (1953-1961); born in Kimberly.

Walkara (1808-1855) Ute Chief known as Walker who led raids against U.S. troops; the Walker War (1853-1854) ended after peace talks with Brigham Young; born near Utah Lake.

Karen Shepherd (1940-) Women's rights advocate; represented Utah in the U.S. Congress (1993-1995); born in Silver City, New Mexico.

Brigham Young (1801-1877) Mormon leader who brought the first group of settlers to Utah in 1847; founded Salt Lake City; served as first governor of the Utah Territory (1849-1857); born in Whittingham, Vermont.

Steve Young (1961-) Great-great-grandson of Brigham Young; quarterback who helped the San Francisco 49ers win three Super Bowl championships (1989, 1990, 1995); born in Salt Lake City.

Words to Know

atomic bomb (uh-TOM-ik BOM)—a powerful explosive that destroys large areas; it leaves behind harmful elements after it explodes.

irrigate (IHR-uh-gate)—to supply dry land with water through ditches, pipes, or streams

low-sulfur coal (LOH-suhl-fur KOHL)—a kind of coal that pollutes less than other coal

Mormon (MOR-muhn)—a member of The Church of Jesus Christ of Latter-day Saints

Olympic Games (oh-LIM-pik GAMES)— sports contests among athletes from many nations

realty (REE-uhl-tee)—the business of buying and selling land and buildings

reservation (rez-ur-VAY-shuhn)—land set aside for use by Native Americans

tram (TRAM)—an enclosed car that moves through the air along a heavy cable

uranium (yu-RAY-nee-uhm)—a metal used in weapons and in power plants

To Learn More

Doubleday, Veronica. *Salt Lake City*. New York: Dillon Press, 1994.

Fradin, Dennis Brindell. *Utah*. From Sea to Shining Sea. Chicago: Children's Press, 1993.

McCormick, John. *The Utah Adventure: History of a Centennial State*. Layton, Utah: Gibbs Smith, 1997.

Thompson, Kathleen. *Utah*. Portrait of America. Austin, Tex.: Raintree Steck-Vaughn Publishers, 1996.

Internet Sites

Excite Travel: Utah, United States
http://city.net/countries/united_states/utah

The Greatest Snow on Earth!
http://www.skiutah.com/greatest.htm

TRAVEL.org Utah
http://travel.org/utah.html

Utah Travel and Adventure Online
http://www.utah.com

Useful Addresses

Anasazi Indian Village State Park
P.O. Box 1329
Boulder, UT 84716-1393

Golden Spike National Historic Site
P.O. Box 897
Brigham City, UT 84302

Historic Temple Square—Public Relations
50 West North Temple Street
Salt Lake City, UT 84150

Park City Silver Mine
P.O. Box 3178
Park City, UT 84060

Utah State Historical Society
300 Rio Grande
Salt Lake City, UT 84101

Zion National Park
National Park Service
Springdale, UT 84767-1099

Index